Killers On The Street

All rights reserved. No part of this publication may be copied or reproduced, Distributed or transmitted in any form or by electronic or mechanical means, without prior written permission of the publisher except in the case of brief quotations embodied in the critical reviews and certain other noncommercial uses permitted by copyright law.

Written by K. C. Anthony
Illustrations by K. C. Anthony
Proofing PSP Proofreading
Paperback: 978-1-964744-40-7 ISBN
ebook: 978-1-9647-44-41-4
Library of Congress Control Number 2024913070
Copyright 2024 by © Kevin C. Anthony.

Prime seven Media, 518 Landmann. St. Tomah City W154660

Index

Page ....*The Intention*................ *1-4*

Page ....*Awareness*................... *5-10*

Page ....*The Dangers*................ *11-15*

Page ....*Consequences*................ *16-22*

Page ....*Face Your Facts*.............. *23-26*

Page ....*What is the Truth*............... *27*

1. The Intention

Living in today's world as a young person can be a daunting thing. There are many pitfalls and traps that tend to steer young people into the worst kind of direction. Drinking alcohol, smoking and drug abuse in any form, are just some of the traps that so many young people fall prey to. However, there are some advantages to being a young person in this day and age; especially when leaving school. There is more freedom of choice and the right to make life changing decisions but more importantly, there are more opportunities to be all that you want to be in life. Whatever your goals are now or may be in the future, your freedom of choice starts here. There are no short cuts to success by any means and what you do at any stage in your life has a very real effect on the direction you may go from that point.

Matt, Geoff and Liam are typical young people growing up in a world that has many pitfalls and traps. It is these pitfalls and traps that often seem irresistible to young people. In reality, they serve only to lure a person away from living their life.

Liam **Geoff**

Hi Geoff, hi Liam. Where are you off to?

Matt

We're off into town. Some of the guys are there. Why don't you meet up with us later? It should be good fun.

Later that day, Matt catches up with his pal Geoff and a few others, and it's not long before a hand full of pills and other harmful substances emerge among the group. Matt has the choice of doing the same thing as others but chooses to stay safe and in control of himself.

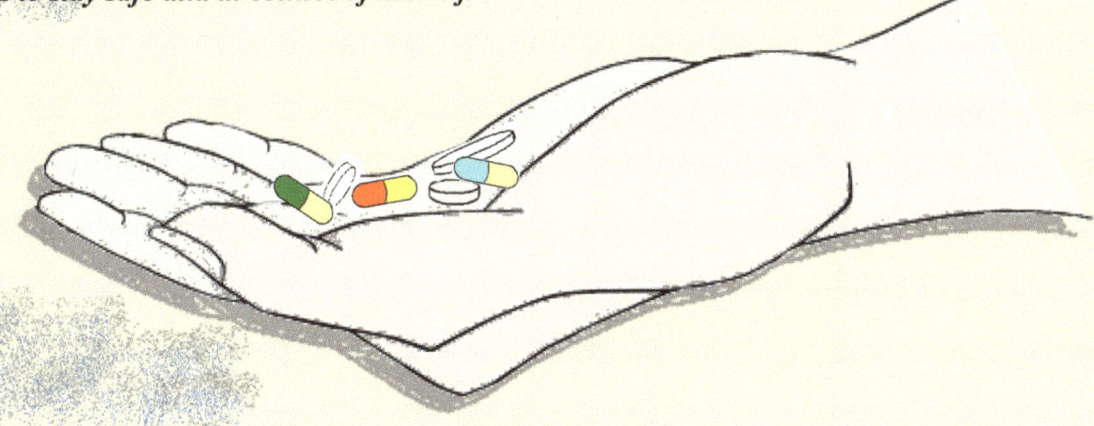

Whether any of your choices are right or wrong, drug-taking can have a lasting effect in all areas of your life. In short, your choice to take a drug can make all the difference between living a life around drug use or a life that has no room for that kind of negativity.

3. The Intention

Linda's conversation with Matt is also cut short when her friend Gemma swiftly drags her way out of Ned's company. Ned meanwhile, has an idea or two in order to influence his friend into doing the same thing as he does.

Ned: Why don't you just relax and take some of this? You'll not want to think about all that studying or training for work! You don't have to take anything now, but you could come down to Geoff's tomorrow instead and check it out then. What do you think?

Matt: 'Mmm, it's your choice to take stuff, but for me, risking a trip to the hospital or worse is not really something I want to do mate. Don't you think you might be taking a risk each time you take something to get high? I was thinking of calling over to Geoff's tomorrow anyway but I'm not going to take anything. It's just not for me, Ned.

Just because you can't see what a drug can do to your mind or to your body, it doesn't mean that there is no damage - nor does it mean any damage is short-lived. Damage done to your mind by drug use is usually irreversible.

Ned: Risks? What risks? I'm used to it now. There's probably less chance of anything happening to me now.

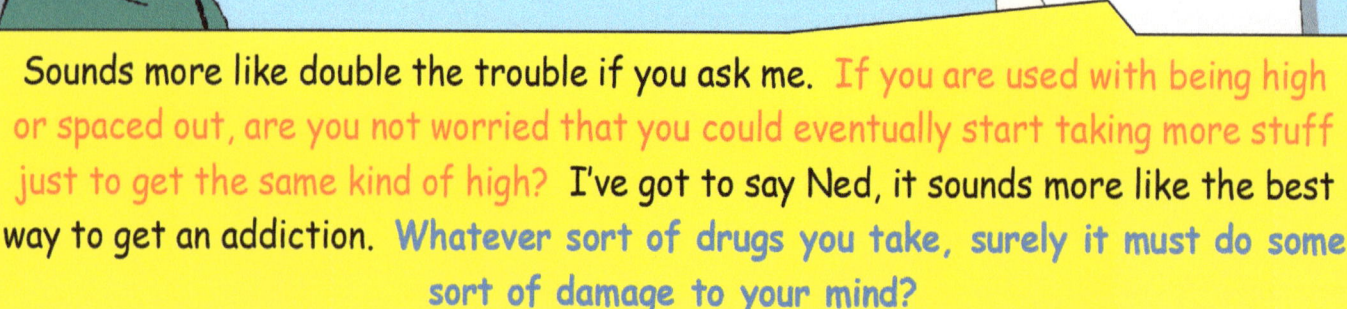

Matt: Sounds more like double the trouble if you ask me. If you are used with being high or spaced out, are you not worried that you could eventually start taking more stuff just to get the same kind of high? I've got to say Ned, it sounds more like the best way to get an addiction. Whatever sort of drugs you take, surely it must do some sort of damage to your mind?

Being used to the effects of a drug does not mean there isn't any damage done to your mind or to other parts of your body. The more potent a drug is, the greater the risk to your mental and physical health. If those things can be greatly affected, then what other damage can drug taking cause to your life?

4. The Intention

A Few Days Later

Gemma: Did you see Ned the other day? Don't know what he'd taken, but I noticed he looked really out of it.

If it's a buzz he wants, he should stick a wasp's nest down his pants.

I just don't get it; there are lots of things to do that don't involve being wasted or being out of control.

Linda: Maybe Ned thinks that most people do what he does. If that's the case, I'm glad to disappoint him. Thankfully I've got my own ideas of what's right for me and they definitely don't include swallowing drugs.

There are many truer words spoken in jest and although Linda teases her friend about Ned, the reality of drug use for kicks is no laughing matter.

Linda: I doubt Ned would ever be able to do any sort of work without having a serious accident. Can you imagine if he was an electrician or a window cleaner?

Gemma: Now that's a scary thought. That would make him even more of a risk to everyone, including himself. There are some people who are happy to believe myths about being able to stay in control when affected by a drug. The fact is, it's impossible to stay in control when your whole understanding of reality is affected.

The girls continue their conversation and share their thoughts on a serious level.

5. Awareness

> Did you read about that rock star that was always getting high before going on stage? I heard he recently caused some of the fans to get hurt when he jumped into the audience. He obviously didn't think about what he was doing.
>
> Apparently, he didn't realise how far he was going at the time or just how dangerous his actions were to others around him. I think his drug fuelled actions have made him look like a total idiot as well.
>
> *That just shows how others nearby can be hurt when someone's mind is affected by a drug.*

Nobody sets out to have an addiction, but how many of those people have said at some point; *"I know when to stop"* or *"It will never happen to me"* or even, *"I can control what I'm doing."* There is no guide as to how quickly a drug can take hold, or how out of control it can make you, but the effects are never good for anyone.

Gemma

> Get this, my brother said when his best friend used to get high all of the time, and eventually he started taking more stuff just to get the same effect as before. I think he said that also caused problems for him and his family. My brother reckons that *using any potent drug for long enough could lead to using other kinds of drugs as well.*
>
> I've heard of changing your life, but aren't you supposed to change it for the better.
>
> *So, why would anyone think that an illicit drug is a reasonable thing?*

6. Awareness

Friends and relationships are what we choose them to be and with whom we choose, but what kind of friendship encourages harm in the pursuit of fun?

> Hi Linda, where are you off to? I've been trying to catch up with you since the other day. I'm going into town for a burger. Are you coming?

Matt

> Ok, as long as you're not meeting up with Ned. I just don't trust him, especially when he looks spaced-out. I'm not sure what to expect from him and that makes me feel unsafe around him.

Matt & Linda arrive in town, but are spotted from across the road by Ned.

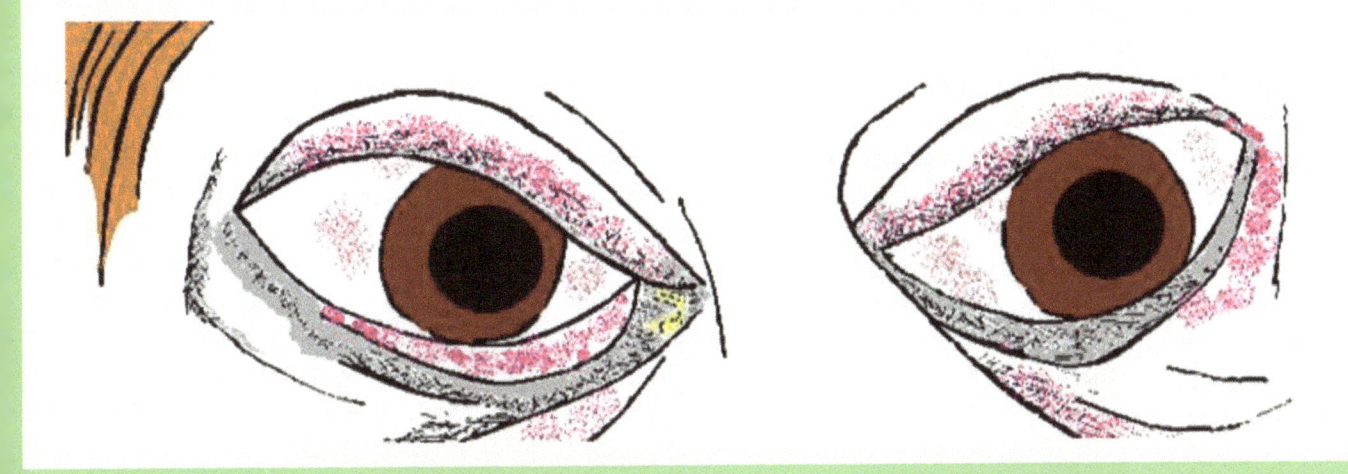

7. Awareness

We could do this at the weekend and ask Gemma, Liam and Ned to come along for a laugh, what do you think?

Linda

I'm always up for a laugh but I don't want to be around Ned.

You might think I'm being stupid but what Ned does is something he chooses for himself and for his own life.

I choose not to be around something that could cause me to get hurt through unpredictable behaviour.

Let's face it, how can anyone be in control of how a drug affects them? Anything might happen.

I just don't trust the sort of things that can happen when drug taking is involved.

When a person's behaviour becomes unpredictable, it can be very unsettling for others who are not into doing the same thing.

8. Awareness

Drug abuse should never be taken lightly, especially when it is pushed onto others. How can someone else's habit affect other people?

Matt

Yeh, I know what you mean. I've seen how unpredictable Ned can be when he's not in his right mind. Your right, **the effects of any drug on a person are unpredictable.** You just can't tell how someone may respond at any point.

T be honest, that's why I never let myself be persuaded into doing drugs just because someone else wants me to.

The way I see it, is that I'm a separate person from Ned and I have my own ideas of what's right for me.

We are all different from one another in many ways, but when it comes to substance abuse, the only guarantee is that their effects are always unpredictable and that can be very disconcerting for others who are not used to seeing drug fuelled behaviour.

We have the ability to outwardly express our thoughts & emotions in different ways (i.e) anger, despair, excitement, displeasure, love and so on. This alone separates us from the animal kingdom along with the ability to control ourselves and behave in a rational way. These things allow us to call ourselves the most intelligent or advanced of creatures. But how rational or advanced is it to slowly kill off or damage your own vital organs with a man-made toxin or poison, and call it recreational fun?

9. Awareness

It's not long before Ned is on the scene, but his idea of a joke on Linda shows no self-control or thought about the danger his actions may pose to others.

Ned

I think I'll go to the loo.

Linda

10. Awareness

Ned: Hi, how's it going Matt? What's up with Linda? She always seems to avoid me when I'm around.

I've half a mind to have a joke on her and put something in her drink. It might be funny. She might even find it funny as well, what do you think?

It is never ok to experiment with drugs but it is even worse to put someone else's health and even the life at risk in the pursuit of what you might call of fun. **Where is the self-control in that?**

"**NO WAY NED!**"   I'm not going to let you do that. It's the dumbest if not the most dangerous thing you could do. Don't you get it? What if she has a bad reaction, or worse? How do you know that she's not already taking medication's for an illness or something? If something were to happen to her, do you think her family would treat it as just having a laugh? Don't think the police would see it as harmless fun either. Do you?

After Matt's warning, Ned reluctantly agrees not to continue his stupid and very dangerous prank but, when no one is looking he still spikes Linda's drink.

11. The Dangers

Linda returns to the table and continues her drink, unaware of what Ned has done or the danger she is in.

As the drug begins to work on Linda, her face becomes flushed and she suddenly begins to feel very unwell. Linda feels something is wrong and begins to panic. Matt is quick to call an ambulance, but before it arrives, Linda collapses and falls to the floor. Who knows what damage Ned's drug has done to Linda's brain or other vital organs.

Ned suddenly remembers what Matt had been saying earlier about the consequences of his actions and quickly disappears from the scene.

12. The Dangers

Drug taking affects more than just the individuals that take them or their own families. It has an effect on the whole of your community in one way or another. **If someone else's drug abuse accidently harms another person, should it be excused as simply being unfortunate or carelessness?**

A couple of weeks later, Ned and Geoff are sitting in a public place, where traces of other drug use are easily found.

Geoff: By the way Ned, Linda is out of hospital now. Word is, she had a very bad reaction to whatever you put in her drink. Truth told, it could have turned out far worse than it did, especially for her and her family.

I don't think her parents have ever been so gutted at what has happened to their daughter. I doubt it's something they'll ever forget in a hurry.

Ned: I didn't think it would have had that effect on her and I didn't expect her to be quite so ill. It was just a joke really. How was I supposed to know that she would have had such a bad reaction?

13. The Dangers

In the street or area where you live, most people may know and trust each other through growing up together, or simply through being neighbours. It is this trust that is referred to as "the fabric of society." It is this trust that helps us to feel safe and secure in the place where we live. It is this trust that helps keep towns, cities and small communities together. So how can the actions or judgements of someone under the influence of a drug; ever be trusted?

Ned: Look Geoff, someone forgot to lock up their bike. Maybe that's our gain and their loss. What do you think?

Geoff: Just at the right time eh? I don't care who it belongs too, we can get what we need if we take it.

Ned   Matt   Geoff

If alcohol and drugs make you lose the plot or do desperate things to fuel a habit, then what else might they do to you and the rest of your life before they take over completely?

14. The Dangers

When under the influence of drugs, sound judgment is impaired and the way you are with others is never right. It is at such times like these that the simplest of answers to the simplest of situations can easily become something far worse than it ever needed to be. It would be fair to say that if you mess with your mind, you're messing with your life or even the lives of others in your path.

When Ned' and Geoff's boyish antics suddenly turn sour, a nightmare for the man and his family begins when violence enters the equation and Ned attack's the man.

"Hey what do you think you're doing? Leave the bike where it is and clear off before I call the police."

Victim

"I don't think so, mate. It probably doesn't belong to you, anyway, so back off unless you're looking for a fight.

Ned

15. The Dangers

It is no joke being a victim of any sort of crime. If you or a family member are hurt or even die as a result of someone's drug fuelled antics, the effects of that are far reaching for everyone. If you were faced with such a thing, **"how would it affect you and, who or what would you blame?** The person who supplied the drugs in the first place, perhaps the person who chose to take them or maybe you would blame the drugs that were taken?

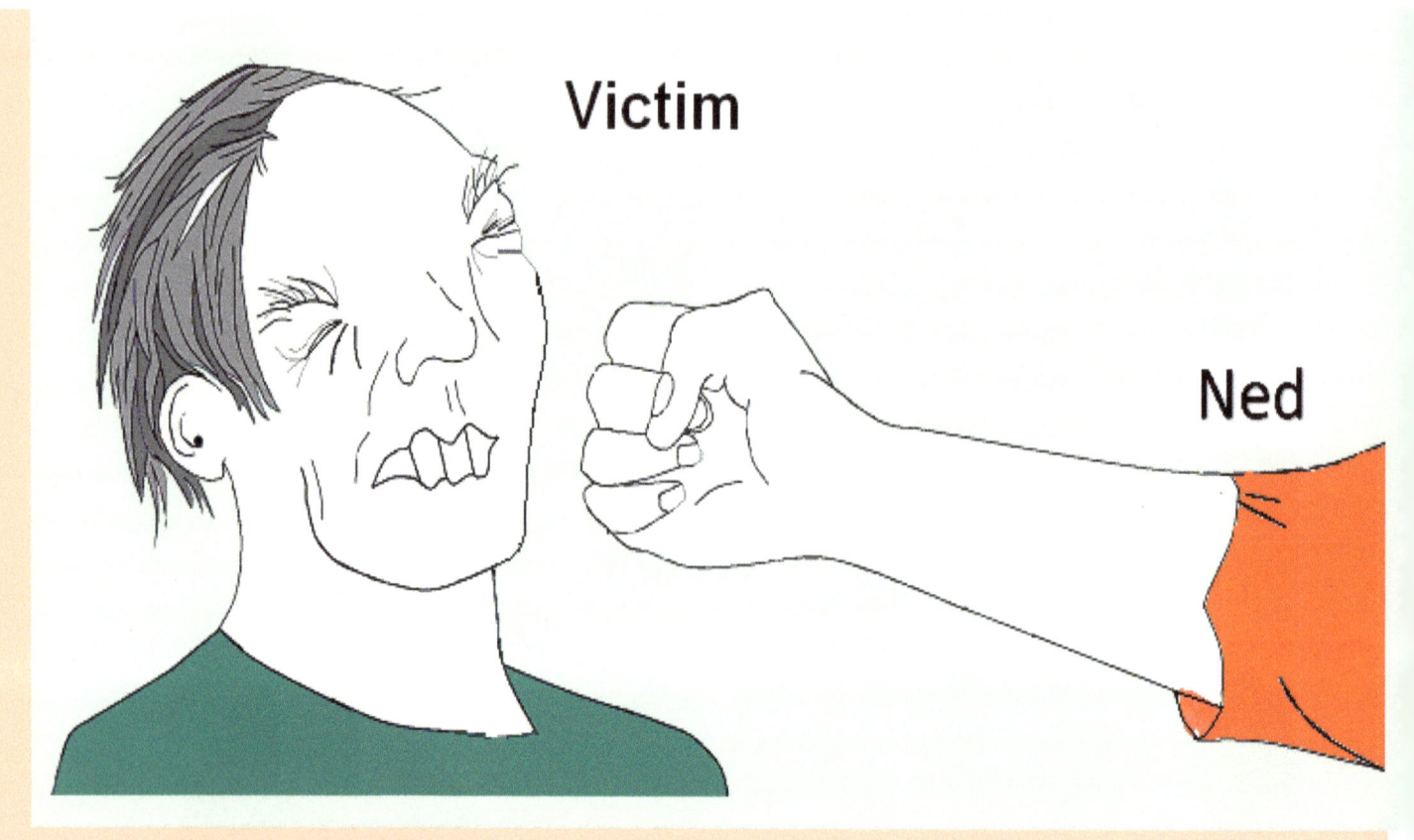

The situation suddenly turns violent and Matt has no chance to intervene. Ned and Geoff bring the man to the ground and leave him there bleeding while they quickly scarper around the corner. Matt is in disbelief of what had just happened and calls an ambulance.

For every action there is a reaction and if your actions speak louder than words, then the consequences of reckless actions should never be ignored. What should we expect to see happen if we behave badly towards others, and is it really worth the trouble?

The injured man is taken to the hospital, but his life could easily have been in the balance had Ned and Geoff continued their violent behaviour. The police are eventually on the scene and it will not take them long to catch Ned or Geoff.

16. Consequences

The lives of the man and his family are changed for ever in many ways. Fear has caused problems for the children and made life even harder for the family to cope with. In essence, the drug fuelled mind set and actions of another person has brought much turmoil into the lives of other innocent people.

Victim's family

This could have a long-term effect on us all.

How on earth will we manage while their Dad is unable to work?

Our lives have been made so much harder.

When drug taking touches other lives, there is no limit as to how many people it hurts. In many cases like this one, the effects of someone's drug fuelled antics can last a life time for others.

I'm frightened to go anywhere without Mum now. Maybe those lads will come back to hurt us.

I'm unsure of everyone.

17. Consequences

Latterly, all the lads end up back at Ned's house and talk about what had happened earlier with the man. As Ned begins to speak, it becomes more apparent to Matt that Ned's drug fuelled mind had caused him to experience paranoia and was likely to be the reason for his violent outburst towards the man.

> I didn't actually mean to go that far. I would have left the bike but I thought he was going to grab me or something and that took me by surprise. It all just spiralled out of control somehow.
>
> Ok, I know I might have got it a bit wrong but surely you can see why I might have jumped the gun?
>
> Honestly, I didn't realise how far I was going until it was too late.

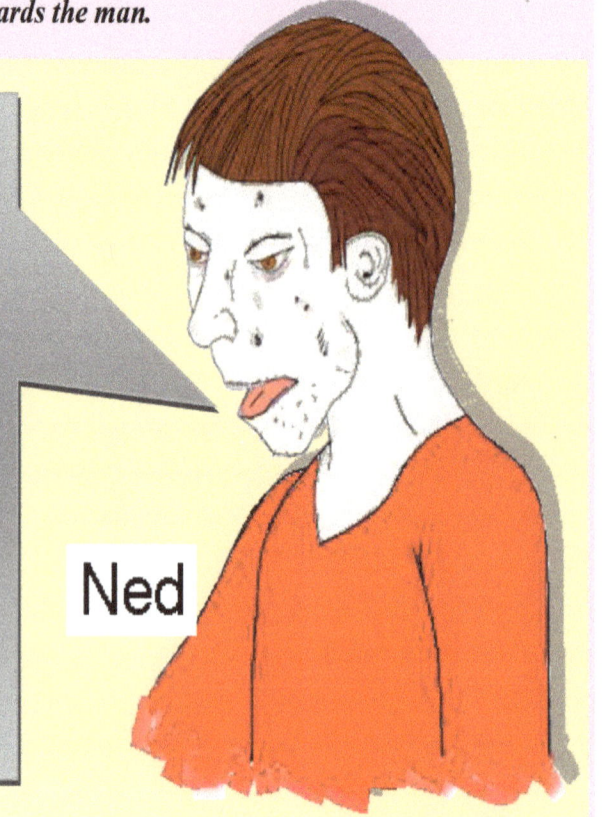

Ned

There can never be any excuse for harming others, not least when under the influence of any substance.

What a couple of idiots! It seems even a house brick might have more brain cells than these two.

Matt

> You idiots, you've seriously hurt that guy! **What were you thinking?** He only wanted to stop you from stealing his bike. You just had to go one step further. Both of you must be on a mission to get locked up.
>
> Surely you must now see how your habit can touch other ordinary lives around here? Not to mention the effect it's having on your own lives.

Matt hopes the lads will finally get the message about being out of control through and the consequences of their drug fuelled actions.

18. Consequences

As Matt Pauses for thought, the reality of everything hits him like a bomb shell

Matt

It just goes to show how drugs can take you to a point of no return and when it comes to being out of control for just a moment, it can have a huge effect on what happens next in your life.

Some lifestyle that is...

In life, there are many choices to make and some more important than others. If your choices are based on positive elements that you truly believe in; then it is more likely that your choices are going to be the right one's for you.

Mate, I just don't get why you would want to be so messed up. Let's face it lads, since when is it cool to keep your brain in the clouds or not have a clue?

Maybe you need to get a grip lads "BEFORE IT'S TOO LATE."

Getting out of it and putting yourself, your freedom and others at risk is just not worth it?

"Surely you can see that now"?

19. Consequences

Matt leaves Ned and Geoff to do some thinking. But Ned still chooses not to get real with any of his thoughts. However, Geoff begins to understand how drug taking may be having an impact on his life.

Geoff: My dad hates my life style, he keeps telling me that getting high is a mugs game. He reckons I should pack it in and risk getting some qualification instead of an addiction or a sentence.

I'm starting to think that maybe he's right.

Let's face it, getting high has never improved anything for me. I've got less money in my pocket and that just doesn't help at all.

When it comes to the cost of drug abuse, life is anything but easy. Obviously, there is the physical harm to yourself but what effect do they have on being successful in other areas of your life such as the career or job front? What affect can drug abuse have on personal things in your life?

Ned: Aah………. Maybe you're just over reacting because of what happened earlier with that guy. Maybe Matt & your dad have got it all wrong. What does Matt know anyway? I think I would know if my brain was starting to getting screwed-up wouldn't you? Why don't you relax and stop thinking.

It would be fair to say that what may be right for one person is not always right for another. We each have the power to shape and change our lives into what we want it to be by using what we believe is right for us. But how positive or productive is it to bringing any sort of drug use into your life? The longer drug abuse stays in someone's life, the less likely they are to truly succeed in what they want. (What would you want to be known for in your life?)

20. Consequences

After leaving Ned's house with a pocket full of stuff, Geoff is spotted by the police at the end of the road and they are keen to question him.

Oh no! "Just my luck, if he searches me, I'm done"

Good evening young man I'd like to have a word with you?

Geoff has a good reason for not wanting to be searched and quickly turns tail in a desperate bid to escape the police. It's not long before he's caught and his reasons for running become quite clear down at the station.

School Yard

21. Consequences

Geoff's habit has led him into a bad situation. The value of his freedom alone will soon become apparent when the cell door is slammed shut.

Geoff

There is always a price to pay when drug use is a factor and the price is always your health in one way or another.

Should you not also consider the price to your family if you were to die as a result of your drug experimenting?

The Law

Mr Parker, Drug abuse is not just about the affect it has on you. It is also about how your community is affected, especially if an innocent person is harmed as a result of your behaviour and actions. A person's behaviour and actions can be far reaching into the lives of others as well as your own - and that is not a good thing by any standard. In this case, your actions have led you to harm another person and ultimately led you here. You should spend time to think about this and how drug use affects more than just yourself. "TAKE HIM DOWN".

Getting high was never going to do me any favours in the long run.

I wish I had stopped and thought about my actions in the first place.

22. Consequences

Days Later

Ned is found lying on the sofa unconscious as a result of an over doze of poison in his body. Whoever gave Ned his drugs, will never take responsibility for the harm their drugs have caused. For the dealer, it will be business as usual regardless of what happens to Ned.

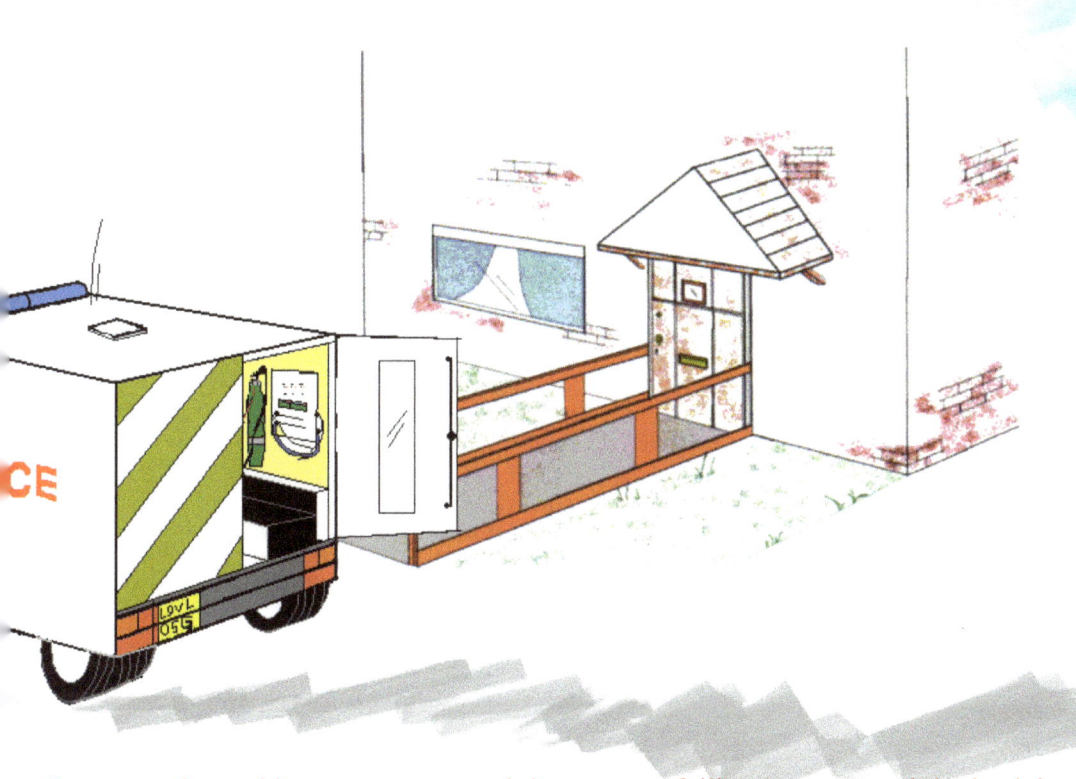

For some, drug taking may never result in an organ failing or even result in death but since when does it mean that the likelihood of these things happening are diminished for anyone else? Since when does it mean that drug-taking cannot cause mental illness? We all make mistakes in our life time, but how dangerous do the consequences of your choice have to be before you realize how costly they can be?

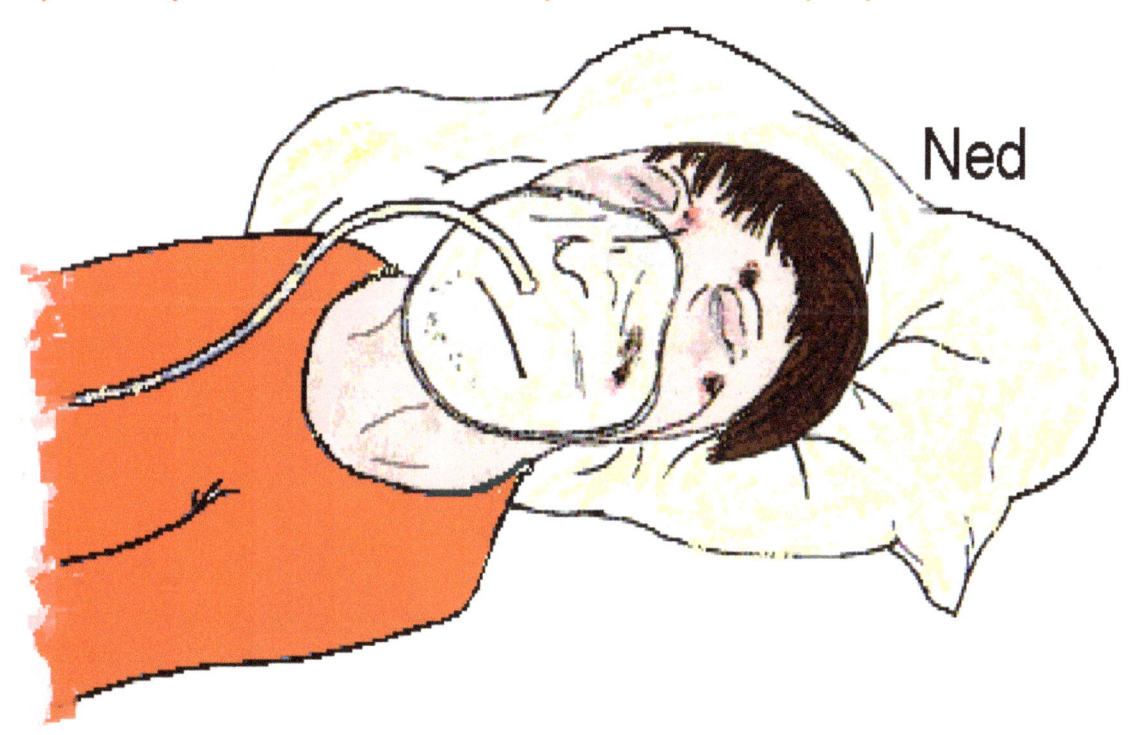

Ned

By the time the ambulance reaches the hospital, Ned has already paid the price for his habit. His family are distraught.

23. Face Your Facts

It is every parent's nightmare to lose a son or daughter, especially through something as needless as drug use. If you were a parent, who would you blame? Would you blame "THE PUSHER" for supplying your child or would you blame "THE DRUGS THEY USED"? "How would you feel"?

Life is what you choose it to be through actions and choices. The choice to use any potent or illicit drug is simply an easy way to waste your life or end it.

Ned's untimely death is enough to make all his friends think about the dangers of using an illicit drug.

Liam

Drug taking really did take over his life after all. "ONLY THIS TIME, IT WAS FOR KEEPS"

If Ned had been more aware of the facts about drug use, it might have made him think differently about what he was doing. It might even have saved his life.

24. Face Your Facts

Liam is not the only one to have an opinion and the girls say what they think too.

Gemma: If everybody was more aware of the drug trap there would probably be less fatalities linked to drug taking.
I don't think Ned took the facts of his choice seriously enough. It just may have saved his life in the long run.

Linda: I just can't understand why anyone would choose to do something that can only have the worst effect on a person's life, especially their mental health.

Matt: Yeh, I know what you mean. Where's the sense in slowly damaging your brain and paying for the privilege?

It just goes to show that awareness really is important.

25. Face Your Facts

Freedom of choice is always important; it allows us to grow and expand our horizons. It allows us to make mistakes and learn from them, so that we don't make that same mistake again. But what if that choice involves using an elicit toxin?

Gemma: We make choices about all sorts of things every day, whether they're good or bad, right or wrong but *surely, it makes good sense to stop and think before you act - especially if your choice has a serious health risk attached to it.* Let's face it, would you jump out of a speeding car knowing what the danger to your life would be?

Liam: I get what you mean Gem, experimenting with a drug is like jumping out of a moving car because it's still a crazy gamble with your life.

How scary is that?

Matt: I guess in the end, it's down to the choice of the individual.

Unfortunately, some people choose to find out their mistake the hard way.

26. Face Your Facts

While the conversation flows, everyone agrees that the drug trap is an easy thing to fall into.

Liam: It's so easy to just to follow what someone else is doing so you don't feel like the odd-one out.

Gemma: Making your choice based on what someone else is telling you it should be or because you don't want to be the odd-one out, is all part of the drug trap.

That sort of reminds me of a sheep. I for one make my own choices when it comes to that sort of thing.

There are many things which can stop a person leading a normal life such as a natural illness, being mentally or physically handicapped or even living in a war zone. But if you're not affected by any of those things, why do something that will mess up your mind and ultimately stop you from living a normal life?

Linda: Can't argue with that Gem. I prefer to think for myself too. Feeling pressured into taking something is probably the worst reason to get involved.

What may be right for one person may not be right for another.

It's fair to say that we all make dumb choices from time to time but if you're going to make a mistake then let the mistake be yours without any excuses.

27. What Is The Truth

Drug abuse is not just a problem in Great Britain and the UK, it is a problem that stretches right across the globe to many other countries like Australia, the Americas, the Caribbean, Germany, Africa, Asia, and so on. In 2001 it was documented in a report by the Economic and Social Council in Vienna, that the use of cannabis in Great Britain, Northern Ireland and Greece were lower than that of previous years (1995 or 1998) but that it was still very much a problem in almost every county in comparison to other drugs. The ESC (Economic & Social Council) report for that year shows that some countries like Singapore and Australia had also reported a slight decrease in cannabis abuse but even in that light, we would be foolish to think that such findings are likely to stay the same for any given amount of time, especially with each new generation of young people coming into the world.

Drug abuse refers to more than just cannabis, amphetamines and other elicit or illegal drugs, it refers to alcohol & tobacco's as well as miss-use of prescription and or sport related drugs. In relation to tobacco's, studies in 2003 showed an estimate of over 425 thousand kids becoming regular smokers and out of that estimate, over 135 thousand were more likely to die of their addiction. It would seem that over the years, smoking tobacco's is not just a choice of the individual adult but an unhealthy childhood addiction. In relation to alcohol abuse, the statistics that link alcohol with serious injuries, broken homes, and very bad health problems are alarming. An NHS report shows a survey for 2007 reveals an alarming alcohol related death figure of 6,541 in England alone. In relation other recent research on drug & alcohol abuse at home and abroad, depending on how people live, it would seem that alcohol abuse is the one of the worst trends among schoolchildren in Europe even today. This alone suggests a worsening problem of alcohol & drug crime among juvenile and young people since 2003.

Taking drugs or mixing them with alcohol may be a common or acceptable thing to do for some but it is that kind of relaxed attitude to alcohol and drug use as a whole, that many young people tend to ignore the health risks when it comes to the drugs and drink culture. The whole problem of drug abuse will remain a problem though out the world until it is eradicated and perhaps the only way for that to happen is to be aware and to think before acting.

Milton Keynes UK
Ingram Content Group UK Ltd.
UKHW050003201124
451363UK00017B/232